Clara Barton
Spirit of the
American Red Cross

written by
Patricia Lakin

illustrated by
Simon Sullivan

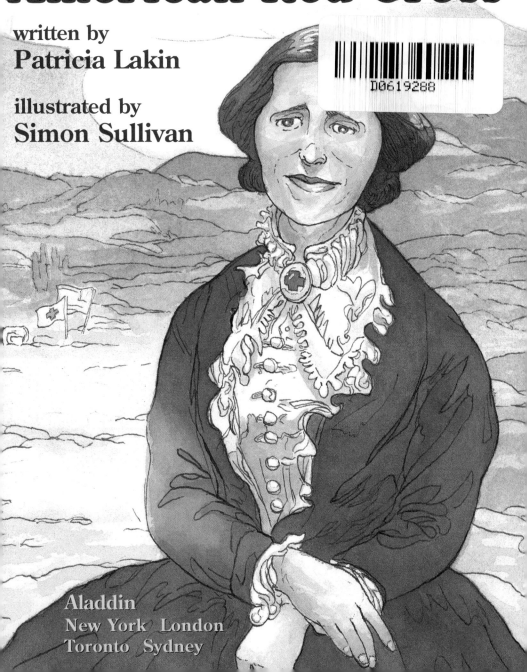

Aladdin
New York London
Toronto Sydney

To George Blinick, this one's for you!
—P. L.

For Laurel —S. S.

The author's main source of information was Elizabeth Brown Pryor's *Clara Barton, Professional Angel* (University of Pennsylvania Press, Philadelphia, 1987).

First Aladdin Paperbacks edition August 2004
Text copyright © 2004 by Patricia Lakin
Illustrations copyright © 2004 by Simon Sullivan

ALADDIN PAPERBACKS
An imprint of Simon & Schuster Children's Publishing Division
1230 Avenue of the Americas, New York, NY 10020

READY-TO-READ is a registered trademark of Simon & Schuster.

Book design by Lisa Vega
The text of this book was set in Century Old Style.

Printed in the United States of America
14 16 18 20 19 17 15 13

Library of Congress Cataloging-in-Publication Data
Lakin, Patricia, 1944-
Clara Barton : spirit of the American Red Cross / by Patricia Lakin ; illustrated by Simon
Sullivan.— 1st Aladdin Paperbacks ed. p. cm.—(Ready-to-read stories of famous Americans)
Summary: A brief biography of the woman who overcame her shyness to become a teacher,
a nurse during the Civil War, and founder of the American Red Cross.
1. Barton, Clara, 1821-1912—Juvenile literature. 2. American Red Cross—Biography—
Juvenile literature. 3. Nurses—UnitedStates—Biography—Juvenile literature. 4. United States
History—Civil War, 1861-1865—Medical care—Juvenile literature. [1. Barton, Clara,
1821-1912. 2. Nurses. 3. American National Red Cross. 4. Women—Biography.]
I. Sullivan, Simon, ill. II. Title. III. Series.
HV569.B3L35 2004
361.7'634'092—dc22
2003018974
ISBN 978-0-689-86513-8 (Aladdin pbk.)
ISBN 978-0-689-86514-5 (Aladdin Library Edition)
0121 LAK

Chapter 1
Who Was Clara Barton?

Floods! Fires! Earthquakes! Disease!
When any kind of disaster happens in
the United States, one group always
rushes in to help. It is the American Red
Cross. And Clara Barton is the one to
thank. She formed the American Red
Cross in 1881.

Clara traveled widely, met kings and queens, and was world famous. But when she was growing up, it seemed unlikely that Clara would ever leave her rural home in North Oxford, Massachusetts. She was painfully shy as a child and even as a young adult.

Clara was born on Christmas Day in 1821. The Bartons already had four children. For Clara, having four much older siblings was both good and bad.

On the positive side, her sister Sally introduced her to books. Clara loved reading and said that she could never remember not being able to read. Her older brothers, Stephen and David, dared Clara to join in their sports games. When she was only five, they dared her to ride a horse bareback. Clara took on all of their wild challenges eagerly. She proved to be good at sports and horseback riding.

But there was a negative side to being the youngest. Clara's brothers and sisters often told her what to do. Clara said that she felt as if she had six parents instead of two. And the family often teased Clara by asking her questions about things she couldn't possibly know.

Clara was highly sensitive. That trait, plus the bossing and teasing she suffered, kept her self-confidence very low.

Clara felt that she was unattractive. She had a big, round face and was also plump. She was short for her age. After the age of nine, she grew only one inch. Clara's one good feature was her thick, brown hair. But Clara's mother kept it cut very short so it wouldn't need much care.

As time passed, Clara withdrew more and more. At home Clara asked for nothing. She didn't ask to have her matted hair combed out. She didn't ask for new shoes or dresses when her old ones no longer fit properly.

But Clara did have some moments of feeling valued. When she was eleven years old, her brother David fell and was badly injured. The injury made him very weak and sick. The doctor gave up hope. Clara didn't. She cared for David for the two years it took for him to recover. Clara was beginning to see that when she was "needed" she felt better about herself. But she wasn't always needed and her self-confidence remained very low. Clara's family worried about their shy, withdrawn teenage daughter.

Chapter 2
Clara's Career and Her "Boys"

Clara's mother came to the rescue. She met a man who thought that by feeling a person's head he could "read" their strengths and their weaknesses. Not everyone thought his method worked. But he was right about seventeen-year-old Clara. He said that Clara was too sensitive for her own good. He also thought she'd make a great teacher. Clara's family then urged her to teach summer school in North Oxford.

Mrs. Barton wanted young-looking Clara to appear as mature as possible. She had a beautiful green dress made for Clara to wear. But the dress didn't bring Clara success. Clara's way with her students did.

Clara's experience with her older brothers was one reason for her success. When her male students played their sports games, Clara joined in. Her "boys" were impressed with their teacher's talents.

Her siblings' teasing may have been another key to Clara's success. Clara treated her students as she wished she had been treated—with respect. She made learning fun and exciting. The summer school was a huge success. And Clara was gaining self-confidence.

In 1851 Clara moved to Bordentown, New Jersey, and took another teaching job. Her success followed her. After three years of teaching, a job opened to head her school.

Clara wanted the position. But at that time, people didn't think women were as capable as men. A man who had never taught at the school was chosen instead of Clara. So Clara left and moved to Washington, D.C. She took a job with the U.S. government. She worked for the Patent Office and granted permits to people who had created new inventions.

It was not long before trouble loomed in the country. The people in the northern states thought slavery was wrong. Southerners disagreed and wanted to form a separate country. In April of 1861, the argument grew into the Civil War. Soldiers who fought for the North, the Union Army, arrived in Washington, D.C. Clara was astonished to see some of her former students. Her "boys" were now soldiers! Clara felt she had to help them.

She wrote to friends and relatives in Massachusetts and New Jersey asking for clothes, food, and medicine. Packages came pouring in. Her supplies soon filled three warehouses! She gave out the supplies as fast as they came in.

As the battles began, the wounded were sent back to Washington for medical help. But it took a long time to get the men there. Clara saw that these soldiers' wounds were worse than they should have been. The soldiers needed medical help right after the battles, not weeks later. Clara realized she and her supplies were *really* needed close to the fighting. Again, she had to battle the public's view not only of women's abilities, but women's courage as well. Clara tried for months to get a permit to go to the battlefields.

She had no luck. Finally, in July of 1862, she met with an army colonel. Clara told him she wanted to bring her supplies to the front. He immediately gave Clara a permit. But it was only for the campgrounds where there was no fighting.

Chapter 3
A Homely Angel

At first Clara followed the rules. Then, on a steaming hot August day, Clara heard about a huge battle with many wounded. Clara didn't worry about proper permits. She *had* to go to where she was needed! Clara rode her supply-filled wagon to Cedar Mountain, Virginia.

The battle ended four days before Clara arrived. But badly wounded men were still lying in open fields under the broiling hot sun. Instantly Clara went to work. She cooked food, gave out drinks of water, and ripped cloth for bandages. She wrote down words that dying soldiers wanted to pass on to their families.

Clara worked for days and nights. The doctor in charge looked at Clara Barton and said, "If heaven ever sent out a homely angel, she must be one. . . ."

Clara sided with the North—she did not think slavery was right. But this "angel" didn't take sides when it came to the wounded. After tending the Union soldiers at Cedar Mountain, Clara heard there were some wounded Southern soldiers, called Confederates, nearby. Clara gave her supplies and help to those wounded as well.

23

At the end of August, Clara heard of
another nearby battle, at Bull Run. The
Union wounded had been brought to the
railroad station in Fairfax, Virginia. Clara
arrived by train. She was not prepared
for the sight. In the fields next to the
station she saw thousands of wounded
soldiers, who were covered in filth and
blood.

There were not enough doctors, medical supplies, food, or water. Clara had no training as a nurse. But she bandaged wounds or held men still while a doctor operated. She gently closed the eyes of men who died. She worked for two days straight. But time was running out. A scout rode up and warned Clara and the other workers that the enemy was nearby. He asked if Clara could ride a horse bareback. Thanks to her older brothers, Clara could.

In that case, the scout explained, she would be able to escape more quickly and could stay an extra hour to help the wounded before she'd have to run for her life. Luckily, Clara and the others were able to load all of the wounded onto the train. They pulled out of the station just as the Confederate Army appeared.

In the early morning of September 12, 1862, an army messenger handed Clara a note. It said, "Harper's Ferry—not a moment to be lost." This was the first time the Union Army asked for Clara's help. It was also the first time they'd given her top-secret information. Harpers Ferry, a place sixty-five miles south of Washington, was about to be the scene of a fierce battle. The army wanted Clara there as soon as possible!

After the battle at Harpers Ferry, Clara had no time to rest. She then tended to soldiers after the battle at Antietam. A soldier there begged Clara to remove the bullet from his face. She took out her pocketknife and did as he asked. Later, she held a man's head as she helped him drink some water. As he sipped, his body shook mysteriously. In an instant, he died. Clara looked down and saw why.

There was a gaping hole in her sleeve. A bullet had gone through it. It found its way into the body of the soldier.

Clara didn't run, not then, not ever. She didn't run from bullets whizzing around her or from the enemy on her trail. She said her place was "anywhere between the bullet and the hospital." In April of 1865, the Civil War was over. The North declared victory.

Chapter 4
Speaking Out for the War's Wounded

Clara wasn't paid for the work she did during the Civil War. She was now short of money. Clara wanted to work at something that was important to her. A friend suggested, "Tell the world as you told me . . . of our brave boys in blue."

Clara agreed. She decided to give lectures. She spoke in schools, churches, town halls, and theaters all over the country. She told large audiences about her experiences and the horrors she'd seen in the Civil War. She explained how the lack of medical care and supplies had added to the soldiers' suffering.

These lectures helped Clara make a living. More than that, they made her famous. Soon people all over the world learned of Clara Barton, the "Angel of the Battlefield."

In 1869 Clara decided to travel to
Switzerland to visit friends. When
she arrived, a man named Dr. Appia
came to call. He wanted to meet
this brave "angel." He also told her
of a new organization. It was called
the International Convention of Geneva,
or the International Red Cross.
He told Clara how it had been formed.

Ten years before, in 1859, a Swiss man named Jean Henri Dunant, went to Italy on a business trip. While there, he saw a terrible battle. It left thousands of soldiers badly hurt. Doctors, medical supplies, food, and water were scarce. Dunant and the village women tended to the wounded. As he worked, Dunant heard the village women murmur, *"Tutti fratelli."* They were saying, "All are brothers."

Dunant faced the same horrible conditions that Clara had faced an ocean away. Like Clara, he had the will to change things. But he had one thing Clara didn't. He came from a wealthy family and had money. He decided to form a group of trained volunteers.

These trained volunteers would be able to give care to *any* wounded soldier in wartime. He traveled to many countries telling others of his plan. Dunant wanted as many countries as possible to join. The organization was officially formed in 1863.
To honor Dunant, the organization adopted his country's flag. They made only one change. They reversed the Swiss flag's colors. The symbol became a red cross on a white background. That symbol meant help had arrived. Most important, it was, and still is, help that takes no sides!

When Appia finished his story, Clara
Barton was astounded. She had never
heard of this organization or its work.
Yet thirty-two countries were already
members. Dr. Appia asked for Clara
Barton's help. He wanted her to get the
United States to join. Clara agreed.

Chapter 5
Clara's Vision

While Clara was in Europe, other wars broke out. Clara stayed to help. She worked for the International Red Cross. In 1873, because of her efforts, Clara received an important German award, the Iron Cross. It honored her volunteer nursing work. She was the first American woman to receive this honor.

But her sister Sally's death, in 1874, brought Clara Barton back to America.

Once there, Clara got to work again. She wrote and distributed a pamphlet that described the work of the Red Cross. She wanted as many Americans as possible to know about this organization. Clara formed a large group of like-minded people who wrote letters and contacted government officials. They kept asking for the United States to form an American chapter of the Red Cross.

On May 21, 1881, when she was fifty-nine, Clara Barton's goal was accomplished. The American Red Cross was formed and Clara became its first president. Now she also wanted to expand its work. She felt the Red Cross should help victims of wars *and* natural disasters.

In September 1884, Clara Barton went back to Europe. She had been chosen to represent America at the International Red Cross's Convention. The other members of the organization voted to adopt Clara's ideas. They, too, would help victims of natural disasters.

Clara established the Red Cross's headquarters close to Washington, D.C., in Glen Echo, Maryland. She worked tirelessly. Clara led the Red Cross to help the flood victims of Johnstown, Pennsylvania. Her organization helped victims from the deadly hurricane that struck the Sea Islands, off the coast of South Carolina. Clara remained the president of the American Red Cross until 1904, when she was eighty-three. But she still didn't rest.

Clara also wanted to train people to help themselves *after* the Red Cross left an area. She felt that if people knew basic health facts, they could stop a medical problem from getting worse. That knowledge could also stop diseases from spreading. Clara formed the First Aid Society. Its goal was to teach first aid classes. To this day, first aid education is an important part of the work of the American Red Cross.

On April 12, 1912, at the age of ninety, Clara Barton died at her Glen Echo, Maryland, home. She was buried in North Oxford where she was born.

Clara Barton was a shy, sensitive child who was teased and felt unneeded. As an adult, she fought her shyness, her lack of self-worth, and her sensitivity. She fought hunger and filth on the battlefield. She fought public opinion about women's abilities. She took up those fights for one reason—to help others in need. That was why she was such a fearless and tireless worker on the battlefield. That was why she brought the Red Cross to America and expanded its role.

Clara Barton's fighting spirit and her concern for the helpless made her one of the world's most famous humanitarians.

Here is a timeline of Clara Barton's life:

1821   Clara is born on Christmas Day in Massachusetts.

1838   Clara starts teaching summer school in North Oxford, Massachusetts.

1851   Clara's mother dies in July.

1854   Clara begins working in the U.S. Patent Office in Washington, D.C.

1861   Civil War begins in April.

        Clara makes her first trip to the campground with her supplies.

1862   Clara's father dies.

1865   Civil War is over April 9.

        Shortly before he's shot and killed, President Lincoln gives Clara permission to work on locating missing prisoners of war.

        Clara helps uncover the fate of 22,000 soldiers who had been listed as "missing."

1869   Clara departs for Europe. In Switzerland, she meets Dr. Appia of the International Red Cross.

1881   American Red Cross is created on May 21.

1884   Empress Augusta of Germany presents Clara with the Augusta Medal, honoring her humanitarian work.

1898   Clara arrives in Cuba to help the wounded of the Spanish-American War.

1904   Clara resigns as president of the American Red Cross.

1905   Clara creates the First Aid Society.

1907   Clara publishes her autobiography, *The Story of My Childhood*.

1912   Clara dies on April 12 in Glen Echo, Maryland.